METROPOLITAN CENTENARIAN

A Locomotive, its Railway and its Renaissance

Austin Harland

AUTHORS NOTE

In common with most railways of the Victorian era, the story of the Metropolitan is complex and, at times, devious. Only a brief account is given here. Readers requiring more information are advised to consult the books listed in the Bibliography.

I am indebted to many people for their help and encouragement in the production of this booklet. In particular I must express my thanks to Richard Castle, Peter Clarke and Phil Marsh of the Quainton Railway Society, Desmond Croome, Eric Felton and David Hibbert of the London Underground Railway Society, R J Bird of the London Transport Museum, C P Atkins of the National Railway Museum, John Slater of the Railway Magazine, Paul Wilkinson of HM Railway Inspectorate, Alan A Jackson, Frank Goudie, R M Casserley, Sally and Graham Gorton, and the staff at Chesham Library and the London Metropolitan Archives for their assistance. I am also grateful to the photographers whose pictures are credited individually and to Jenny, my wife, for her patience over the many months of preparation.

Published by:
Austin Harland,
19 Poles Hill,
Chesham, HP5 2QR

ISBN 0 9533565 0 7

Printed by:
Orbitpress Ltd.,
11 Market Square,
Chesham, HP5 1HG

Cover illustrations. *Both: T Page*

Front: Metropolitan Railway No. 1 leaves Platform 3 at Quainton Road station with a demonstration goods train, 5th October 1986.

Rear: In the woods above Chawton, Mid-Hants Railway, No. 1 and Southern Railway "S15" No. 506 double-head a train for Alresford.

INTRODUCTION

Known these days merely as the purple line on the London Underground map, the Metropolitan was once a notable railway in its own right.

It was the world's first under-ground railway and, during its 70 years of independence, its tracks were used by express trains from Sheffield and Manchester to London, it ran a regular Pullman service, built some of its own steam locomotives, had a considerable traffic in agricultural produce and other freight and might have formed part of a trunk route from the north of England to the Continent via a tunnel under the Channel. At its peak it extended over fifty miles into rural Buckinghamshire and played a major part in the development of North-west London. It was also the subject of a poem and a television programme by Sir John Betjeman!

Only two ex-Metropolitan locomotives survive today; No. 23, an "A" class engine which saw over 80 years service and is now in retirement at the London Transport Museum, and No. 1, owned by the Quainton Railway Society and based at the Buckinghamshire Railway Centre. It is to commemorate the Centenary of the latter that this booklet has been produced.

Mixed train for Brill? No. 1 with LNER Brake/third, two 6-wheel LNWR vans and a cattle truck in the branch platform at Quainton Road, 29th September 1985.

Photo: T Page

Without cab or side tanks, No. 1 undergoes a static steam test at Quainton on 23rd March 1985. *Photo: G Hamilton*

Your purchase of this booklet is helping to raise funds for the overhaul and restoration of Metropolitan Railway No. 1, hopefully in time to repeat its role of 50 and 100 years ago when the Uxbridge branch celebrates its Centenary in 2004.

Any further assistance you may like to give would be gratefully received. Donations should be sent to:

Quainton Railway Society Ltd.,
Buckinghamshire Railway Centre,
Quainton,
Aylesbury,
HP22 4BY

THE METROPOLITAN RAILWAY

CONCEPTION

Traffic congestion and pollution in London is nothing new. 250 years ago the large numbers of cattle being driven along Oxford Street and Holborn on the way to Smithfield Market caused considerable problems and, in an attempt to alleviate the situation, London's first by-pass was opened in September 1756 from Paddington to Islington. Known as the New Road until 1857, it now forms Marylebone Road, Euston Road and Pentonville Road.

By the 1850's the situation was even worse, with over 750,000 people pouring on to London's crowded streets each day, many through the new railway termini at Paddington, Euston and Kings Cross. A proposal to link these stations with the City by means of an underground Railway had been made in 1845 but it failed to attract sufficient support despite having Robert Stephenson as engineer. Over the next twenty years several other schemes were proposed; Sir Joseph Paxton drew up a grandiose plan for a glass roofed "Grand Circle Railway" with shops and boulevards, echoing his design for the Crystal Palace built a few years earlier, and another suggestion involved laying tracks along the drained bed of the Regent's Canal. The Clerkenwell Improvement Commission, set up in 1840 to deal with the squalor in the valley of the River Fleet which was little more than an open sewer, proposed a central terminus for lines entering London from the north.

In 1853 a proposal, originally called the Bayswater, Paddington and Holborn Bridge Railway, was granted Parliamentary approval as the North Metropolitan Railway for a line from Paddington to King's Cross with John Fowler as engineer. At the same time a revised version of the Fleet valley scheme, known as the City Terminus Company, was being championed by Charles Pearson, Solicitor to the Corporation of the City of London, to link King's Cross with Holborn. The two schemes, combined and reincorporated as the Metropolitan Railway, gained approval on 7th August 1854 for a sub-surface railway from Paddington along the route of the New road. Originally the line was to pass under Bartholomews Hospital and terminate in the basement of the General Post Office at St Martin's-le-Grand but when a deviation was proposed because *"the vibrations from passing trains might interfere with operations and patients"* and permission to pass under Cold Bath Fields Prison refused by the Prison Commissioners, the terminus was moved to Farringdon Street.

Initially progress in raising finance was slow, much to the disgust of the Times which, in 1856, was complaining:

> *"It is rather singular that we, who of all nations are the most fond of travel and who pride ourselves on the facility with which we can circumnavigate the globe, do not yet know how to get from one end of our own metropolis to the other."*

However, by the end of 1859, largely through the efforts of Pearson, the £1,000,000 capital required had been subscribed with the City Corporation and the Great Western Railway contributing £200,000 and £175,000 respectively.

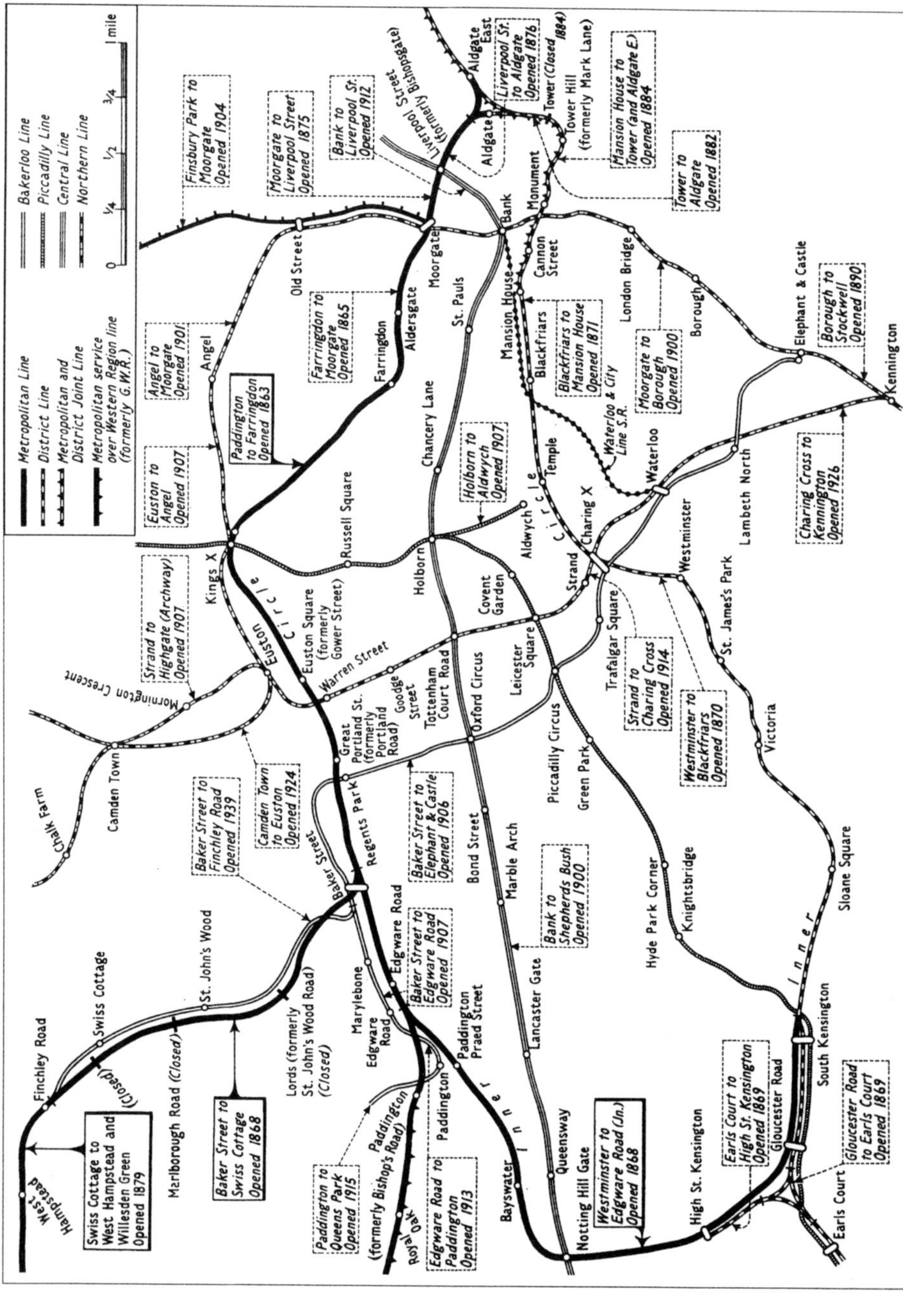

Chronological map of the Circle and other inner London Underground railways before the advent of the Jubilee and Victoria lines.

Map courtesy Railway Magazine

CONSTRUCTION

Contracts were awarded to Smith & Knight for the Euston Square to Paddington section and to John Jay for Euston Square to Victoria Street (later renamed Farringdon Road). Construction was mainly by the "cut and cover" method, i.e. a trench was dug with the sides supported by brick walls and then roofed by a brick arch or cast iron girders with the road surface restored on top, the only genuine tunnel being at Clerkenwell, 728 yards long. Spoil from the excavations was used in the construction of the terraces at Stamford Bridge, the home of Chelsea Football Club. By May 1862 work was sufficiently advanced for a trial trip over the whole line but a month later the Fleet Ditch Sewer burst in flooding the line as far as King's Cross. In December the Board of Trade inspector, Colonel Yolland, demanded some signalling alterations, before he gave his formal approval after a final inspection on 3rd January 1863. Over the next week a service of empty trains was operated to familiarise staff with their duties and to test the signalling system. The Metropolitan was the first railway to be worked throughout on the absolute block system where the tracks were divided into block sections with access to each section controlled by signals. Points and signals were interlocked using block telegraph instruments, another first for the Metropolitan.

On Friday, 9th January, two special trains conveyed over 600 directors, shareholders and guests on a tour of inspection culminating with the customary banquet at Farringdon Street station. Unfortunately Charles Pearson, who had played a major role in establishing the Railway, was not present; he had died on 14th September 1862 but the grateful directors granted his widow an annuity of £250 in appreciation of his services.

The railway opened to the public on Saturday, 10th January 1863 and such crowds attempted to travel on the first day that, despite extra engines and coaches being borrowed from the GWR, booking offices had to be closed at times while the platforms cleared. The following day conditions became so bad that several staff were overcome by the fumes, one being taken to hospital. Nearly 40,000 tickets were issued on the Saturday and the daily average for the first three weeks was over 29,000. The price of shares shot up and City Corporation sold its holding at a handsome profit.

Single fares for the 18 minute journey of 3¾ miles from Paddington to the City were 6d, 4d or 3d depending on the class of travel (1st, 2nd or 3rd) with returns costing 9d, 6d & 5d. In May 1864 the Metropolitan became the first London Railway to issue workmens tickets for travel out at 5.30 or 5.40am and return by any later train at a return fare of 3d. An extension from Farringdon Street to Moorgate Street was opened on 23rd December 1865.

EXPANSION

The success of the Metropolitan led to a profusion of railway projects being proposed, over 250 for London in 1864 alone, and a Parliamentary Committee was set up to review them. Among those approved were the Metropolitan District Railway from South Kensington to Tower Hill, and connections between the Metropolitan and District lines at both ends thus forming an "Inner Circle" linking all existing and proposed main-line termini. The western connection was opened in December 1868 but disputes between the two companies delayed completion of what is now the Circle Line until 1884.

The fourth proposal approved by the Parliamentary Committee in 1864 was the nominally independent Metropolitan & St. John's Wood Railway which opened to Swiss Cottage on 13th April 1868 from a junction at Baker Street. Intended only as a feeder line for the "main line" from Paddington to the City, it was single tracked with severe gradients because of the need for a bridge over the Regent's Canal and ran in tunnel just below ground level with numerous openings left for ventilation. The excavated earth was used to reduce the depth of the Regent's Park lake where 40 people had died when the ice gave way in January 1867. For a short period it operated a "human token" system of train control where no train was allowed on to the sections north and south of the passing loop at St. John's Wood unless a pilot man wearing the appropriate red or blue cap was on the footplate!

Charles Pearson's idea of a central terminus for main-line trains had been blocked by Parliament but several railways used parts of the Metropolitan to reach the City. The Great Western and Great Northern had connections at Paddington and King's Cross respectively from the start, a junction with the London, Chatham & Dover Railway at Farringdon Street was made in January 1866 and with the Midland at St Pancras in July 1868. A connection with the London & North Western Railway at Euston was proposed but never built. To cater for this "foreign" traffic additional tracks, known as the "Widened Lines", were provided between King's Cross and Moorgate.

On 7th August 1872 Sir Edward William Watkin was elected chairman of the Metropolitan and the company's policy underwent a drastic change. He was already Chairman of the South Eastern, and the Manchester, Sheffield & Lincolnshire Railways, a director of the Channel Tunnel Company and had interests in the Chemin de Fer du Nord in France. His dream of a great trunk railway to Paris and beyond may well be apocryphal but he encouraged the South Eastern to make experimental borings near Dover in 1881 and certainly envisaged a through route from the north of England to the south coast. He is quoted as telling Metropolitan shareholders in 1874 that the line would be connected with *"Northampton and Birmingham and many other important towns"* and, in 1888, *"I do not intend to be satisfied . . . without seeing the Metropolitan Railway the grand terminus for a new system of railways through England"*.

The St. John's Wood line fitted in well with these plans and it was extended by stages as a double track reaching Harrow in 1880 and Rickmansworth in 1887. The doubling of the original single line was completed in 1882, although the junction at Baker Street remained single track until the station was rebuilt in 1913. The double track from Rickmansworth to Chalfont Road (now Chalfont & Latimer) and single line to Chesham, where the station and goods yard were aligned to allow a possible further extension to the L&NWR at Tring, were opened in July 1889. Three years later the double track was extended from Chalfont Road through Great Missenden and Wendover but the GWR refused access to its station at Aylesbury and a temporary platform at Brook Street, just short of the junction, was used until the end of 1893.

Considerable areas of surplus land had been acquired in the course of this expansion and a large area to the east of the River Brent was utilised for new carriage shops to relieve congestion at the existing sheds at Farringdon Street and the original depot at Edgware Road. Employees were housed in two streets, designated "A" and "B" until renamed Quainton and Verney Streets in 1903. Shops, a Church and a small school were also provided. The locomotive repair shop, the drawing office and stores department soon followed to the new site and another 40 houses were built in Aylesbury Street. Much of the remaining land was developed for housing by the Surplus Lands Committee, the beginning of what later became known as 'Metro-land'.

The Permanent Way gang relax as L.44 prepares to run round its train at the north end of Aylesbury station on a misty Sunday morning, 21st August 1955.
Photo: A J Reed

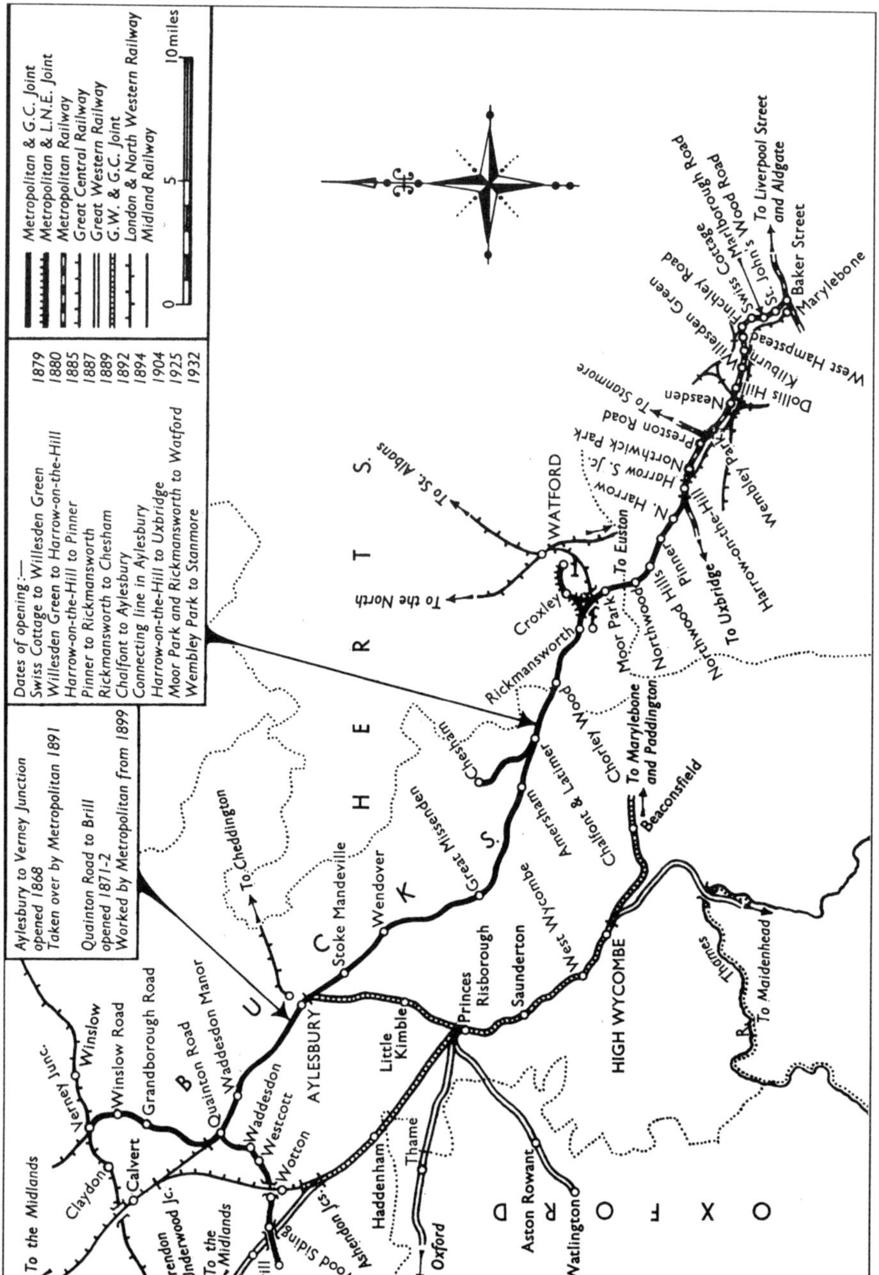

Development of the Metropolitan Railway "Extension line" showing the maximum extent on acquisition by the LPTB in 1933.

Map courtesy Railway Magazine

AYLESBURY & BEYOND

North of Aylesbury the single track of the Aylesbury & Buckingham Railway, opened in September 1868, wended its way through the sparsely populated countryside of North Buckinghamshire to a remote junction with the London & North Western worked line from Bletchley to Bicester. Locomotives and rolling stock were provided by the GWR from the opening and, as Metropolitan locomotives were too heavy for the existing bridges, this continued when the line was taken over by the Metropolitan in 1891. Three years later another dispute between the two companies resulting in the GWR refusing to work the trains and a hurried agreement was made with the L&NWR to provide suitable locomotives until the Metropolitan "D" class engines were introduced in February 1895. Through trains from Baker Street to Verney Junction via Aylesbury and Quainton Road began running from 1st January 1897 after the A&BR line had been doubled.

One of the stations on the A&BR was about a mile from the village of Quainton and, as was customary, had the suffix "Road" added to its name. It was the terminus of the Wotton Tramway, a 6½ mile single track line to Brill, built by the Duke of Buckingham primarily to serve his estate and opened in stages between 1870 and 1872. Originally the only connection with the main line was by means of a wagon turntable and the station comprised a single platform on the village side of the line where the road bridge now stands. The junction was installed and the station rebuilt on the present site when A&BR line was doubled. Operation of the line was taken over by the Oxford & Aylesbury Tramroad Company in October 1894 but their proposal for an extension to Oxford was not carried out and the freehold remained the property of the Duke's successors.

In 1899 an approach by the O&AT management culminated in a letter from John Bell, Watkin's successor, expressing agreement that the Metropolitan would take over the working of the Wotton Tramway at a rental of £600 per year from 1st December 1899 as a temporary measure pending an application for powers to purchase it. Two Manning Wardle 0-6-0 saddle tank locomotives, two passenger cars and a mineral wagon, the personal property of Earl Temple, were purchased for £2375, the rest of the Tramway rolling stock cost £700 but the sale of the line itself never took place and it was operated under the terms of the Bell letter until it closed on 30th November 1935.

THE GREAT CENTRAL

The final decade of the Nineteenth Century was dominated by moves to join the separate parts of Watkin's empire. In January 1890 the Metropolitan granted running powers between Quainton Road and London to the MS&LR and SER in return for contributions towards the cost of the extension northwards to Aylesbury and in 1892 the MS&LR opened a line from Beighton, near Sheffield, to Annesley Junction, north of Nottingham. However, attempts to secure the support of the Great Northern Railway in joining the two failed, as did proposals for joint stations with the L&NWR and Midland at Leicester and Nottingham. Opposition also came from artists living in St. John's Wood and the Marylebone Cricket Club who feared damage to the wicket at Lords!

The fears of the MCC were quickly allayed and a new approach to the GNR led, after protracted negotiations, to agreements regarding running powers and joint ownership of the new station at Nottingham. Despite continued opposition from the artists and the London County Council, Parliamentary approval for the new line was granted in March 1893 and construction began in October 1894 at an estimated cost of £3,182,155 for the 95 miles.

In 1894 the era of Watkin came to end. Aged 73, the pressures of office had affected his health and on 19th May he resigned as Chairman of both companies although he remained a Director until a few months before his death on 13th April 1901. He was succeeded as Chairman of the Metropolitan by John Bell and on the MS&LR the dominant force became the General Manager, William Pollitt. Animosity between these two strong personalities, dating from their days as rivals for promotion as clerks with the MS&LR, led to a period of friction between the two companies which did not end until both retired in 1902.

As construction progressed the MS&LR sought a less provincial title. "Manchester, Sheffield & London" was considered but by popular demand "Great Central Railway" was adopted on 1st August 1897. The official opening of the London extension took place at Marylebone station with suitable ceremony on 9th March 1899 and regular passenger services began on Wednesday, 15th March 1899, although coal and general goods traffic had been carried for some months previously. To avoid congestion on the existing Metropolitan line, an additional pair of tracks was provided for the exclusive use of the MS&LR between Canfield Place, the junction for Marylebone, and Preston Road. These were extended to Harrow in 1901 and leased to the Great Central for 999 years.

RELATIONS, BAD AND GOOD

With John Bell in charge, the Metropolitan began to take a more independent stance. Numerous disputes arose between the two companies with the result that the GCR decided to transfer freight to the GWR at Banbury via a new 8½ mile line from Culworth Junction near Woodford thus avoiding the Metropolitan at Aylesbury altogether. To achieve independent access to London the GCR built a 6½ mile line from Neasden to Northolt and in conjunction with the GWR set up a Joint Committee to construct a line from Northolt to High Wycombe, improve the Princes Risborough line and build a new line to join the GCR at Grendon Underwood, just north of Quainton Road. The Banbury line opened without ceremony in June 1900 but the opening of the Joint line on 2nd April 1906 was marked by a luncheon in the Town Hall given by the High Wycombe Chamber of Commerce. On the same day the newly formed Metropolitan & Great Central Joint Committee took over responsibility for the line from Harrow South Junction to Verney Junction, including the Chesham branch and the Brill Tramway as part of the settlement of the Metropolitan's claim for compensation for the loss of traffic to the High Wycombe route.

Bell's term as Chairman ended in July 1901 due to ill health and Abraham Charles Ellis was appointed general manager. On the GCR, William Pollitt retired in May 1902 and was replaced by Sam Fay who soon formed a cordial relationship with Ellis. One of the first signs of the new mood was an agreement that season tickets could be used on either company's trains.

The Metropolitan was still seeking to be recognised as a main line railway and in June 1910 introduced the first electrically hauled Pullman service in Europe using two 19-seat cars named "Mayflower" and "Galatea" after the contenders in the 1886 Americas Cup yacht races. The first train left Aylesbury for Aldgate at 8.30 each morning (except Sunday) offering first class passengers luxury travel and light refreshments for a supplement of 6d (2½p) from London to Rickmansworth and 1s.0d (5p) beyond. The last train back left Baker Street at 11.35pm and arrived at Aylesbury 80 minutes later, the timetable including the note for Stoke Mandeville *"Calls if required on Saturdays only to set down passengers on notice being given to the guard at the previous station"*. The Pullmans ran until 7th October 1939 when they were withdrawn due to the outbreak of war.

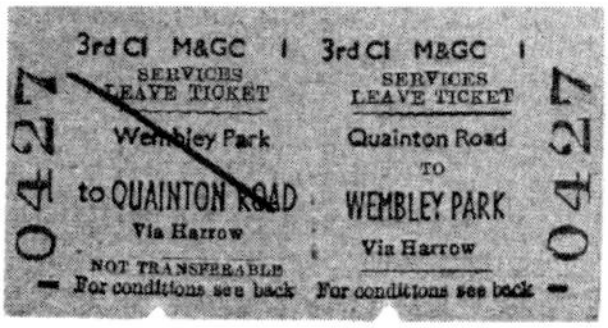

ELECTRIFICATION

Until 1874 smoking was not permitted on Metropolitan trains but this can have had little impact on the conditions caused by operating steam engines within the confines of the tunnels on the original line to the City. It has been said that in early days staff were granted permission to grow beards as protection against smoke and efforts were made to prove the "antiseptic qualities" of the atmosphere but despite various experiments with ventilation tubes and shafts, suggestions of compressed air and water-jet propulsion, it became evident that the answer would be electricity. In one experiment, the original "A" class locomotive No. 1, mounted on blocks, was used to drive a generator powering specially equipped bogie coaches on the short branch at Wembley Park originally built in 1893 to transport materials for Watkin's abortive Tower. Another scheme, in conjunction with the Metropolitan District Railway, used a temporary generating station to supply power via a third rail to a train of six coaches, three owned by each railway, carrying passengers at a special fare of one shilling between High Street, Kensington and Earl's Court.

In 1900 a joint committee set up by the two Railways issued a specification to which nine different contractors submitted tenders. The cheapest, a three-phase, 3,000 volt alternating current system with overhead conductor wires proposed by a Hungarian firm, was recommended by the committee and accepted by the Metropolitan although it varied from the specification. However, the District, which had been taken over by an American group headed by Charles Tyson Yerkes, favoured a low voltage direct current system. The matter was referred to an arbitration tribunal headed by the Hon. Alfred Lyttlelton, K.C. which reported in favour of the d.c. system in December 1901.

The first Metropolitan electric service ran between Baker Street and Uxbridge on 1st January 1905 and the Circle service commenced in September of the same year. From 1st November 1906 electric locomotives replaced steam between Baker Street and Wembley Park, the exchange point subsequently moving to Harrow in July 1908 and Rickmansworth in January 1925. The branches from Moor Park to Watford, and from Wembley Park to Stanmore, now part of the Jubilee Line, were worked by electric trains from the outset.

Two additional tracks on the north side of the line, provided to relieve congestion between Finchley Road and Harrow caused by Uxbridge traffic, were brought into use in stages between 1913 and 1932 but further electrification was delayed by the outbreak of the Second World War and it was not until September 1960 that electric trains reached Chesham and Amersham. Aylesbury trains continued to utilise electric locomotives between Baker Street and Rickmansworth until 9th September 1961 when through running ceased and Amersham became the terminus of the Metropolitan Line.

Right: Three generations of LT motive power: Battery locomotive No. 44 joins No. 1 & L.99 (ex-GWR No. 7715) at the Buckinghamshire Railway Centre, 5th July 1993. *Photo: P Marsh*

LONDON TRANSPORT

With the formation of the London Passenger Transport Board on 1st July 1933 the Metropolitan Railway ceased to exist as a separate entity and with it any remaining aspirations of main-line status. The Brill branch closed to all traffic on 30th November 1935 and passenger trains ceased to run between Quainton Road and Verney Junction in the following year, although goods traffic continued until 1947. From 20th November 1939 the Stanmore branch became part of the Bakerloo line which had been extended from Baker Street to Finchley Road in tunnel and then ran over the centre two of the four Metropolitan tracks to Wembley Park. It became part of the Jubilee line from 1st May 1979.

Under the LPTB some departments from Neasden were moved to the Underground depot at Acton and the steam locomotive running shed was demolished to provide space for the Bakerloo rolling stock. From 1st November 1937 all Metropolitan freight workings were transferred to the LNER which also provided locomotives for passenger trains north of Rickmansworth. Engines of classes "G", "H" and "K" were sold to the LNER and transferred to the Neasden ex-GCR shed. The LPTB staff affected were transferred on loan to the LNER where they continued under their existing conditions of service and rates of pay and were supplied with a distinctive uniform. They were also given the option of returning to the LPTB as vacancies occurred.

By the mid-fifties the LT steam locomotives were considered to be reaching the end of their useful lives and were mainly confined to works and permanent way trains, only occasionally appearing on passenger trains. After a brief and unsuccessful trial with a diesel shunter, they were replaced by ex-GWR pannier tanks which were given numbers in the series L.90 to L.99 and it was one of these, L.94 (ex-GWR No. 7752), which headed the final LT steam working on 6th June 1971.

Class "A" No. 23 has received a new boiler with a closed dome and safety valves above the firebox. The rear of the bunker has been raised but the crew still have little protection from the weather. *Photo: L.U.R.S. collection*

After the addition of a cab, No. 41 spent its final days on the Brill branch where a single coach provided ample accommodation. *Photo: L.U.R.S. collection*

METROPOLITAN LOCOMOTIVES

The original locomotive designed for use on the Metropolitan was the infamous "Fowler's Ghost", a 2-4-0 broad gauge tender engine with 5' 6" driving wheels and 15" dia x 24" stroke outside cylinders designed by John (later Sir John) Fowler who was the engineer in charge of the construction work. To meet the requirement that locomotives would not emit smoke or steam in tunnels the boiler barrel incorporated a chamber containing a large number of firebricks. The theory was that the firebricks would become white hot in normal operation on open sections of track and act as a heat reservoir, releasing heat when the fire was damped down for running in tunnel. It was not a success and in November 1861 the Great Western Railway agreed to work the line supplying both locomotives and carriages. The locomotives were designed by Daniel Gooch and naturally became known as "Metropolitan Tanks". They were not one of his more successful examples as the condensing apparatus fitted to avoid the emission of exhaust steam when working underground proved troublesome and they suffered from water leakage. All were withdrawn within 15 years and their boilers put to stationary use, one being used on Brunel's steamship "Great Eastern". The carriages were eight-wheeled, not bogie, vehicles equipped with coal gas lighting and known as "Long Charleys".

The relationship between the two Companies soon deteriorated resulting in the Great Western withdrawing its stock on 10th August 1863. As mixed gauge track had been installed from the beginning, the Great Northern Railway was able to supply a number of 0-6-0 and 0-4-2 standard gauge tank engines as a temporary measure and carriages were borrowed from the Great Northern and London & North Western Railways. The Metropolitan Railway had been considering purchasing locomotives of its own even before this crisis arose, but it was not until October 1863 that an order was placed with Beyer Peacock & Co. of Gorton Foundry, Manchester for 18 standard gauge 4-4-0T locomotives. Little more than driving wheel diameter was specified by the Metropolitan and the design Beyer Peacock produced was based on a class of 5' 6" gauge locomotives they had built the previous year for the Tudela & Bilbao Railway in Spain.

The first of the new locomotives arrived in June 1864 and by the end of August all 18 had been delivered. They were initially named after characters in Greek or Roman mythology but by 1869 the names had been removed. Robert Harvey Burnett, who had previously been the Beyer Peacock representative in Spain responsible for re-building and testing the T&BR engines on delivery, supervised their entry into traffic and was then appointed Locomotive Superintendent of the Metropolitan, a position he held until he returned to Gorton Foundry as Works Manager in 1872. By 1870 a further 26 engines had been purchased, including 11 which were used on the District Railway until that railway took over its own services in July 1871. These differed only in detail and all 44 engines became known as the "A" class.

Five 0-6-0 tank engines built by the Worcester Engine Company in 1868 for use on the steeply graded St. John's Wood line did not receive a class letter. With their 4' 0"dia wheels, 20"dia x 24" cylinders, and 140lb/in^2 boiler pressure they were found to be too powerful for the light trains then in service and were replaced by the class "A" engines returned from the District. Between 1879 and 1885 22 engines similar to class "A" but with a shorter wheelbase, smaller firebox, larger tanks and other detail differences were introduced by Burnett's successor, Joseph Tomlinson, and designated class "B".

Both class "A" and "B" engines were originally painted bright olive green with black and yellow lining on boiler bands and three panelled side tanks. The chimneys were copper capped and dome covers and brasswork brightly polished but, with the arrival of J. J. Hanbury in 1885, the livery was changed to a dark red with a painted dome and a single large panel on the tank side. A three panelled style was restored with "Metropolitan Railway" in an oval surrounding the engine number on the centre panel in the 1890s.

In anticipation of the extension of the line to Aylesbury in 1892 John Bell, the General Manager, arranged for four 0-4-4 tank engines, similar to the South Eastern Railway's "Q" class designed by James Stirling, to be purchased from Neilson & Co. They were delivered in June 1891 and became class "C". Although fitted with condensing apparatus it is probable they only worked on open sections of the line and the apparatus was eventually removed. They were painted in the dark red, three panelled style with the oval scroll surrounding the number from new.

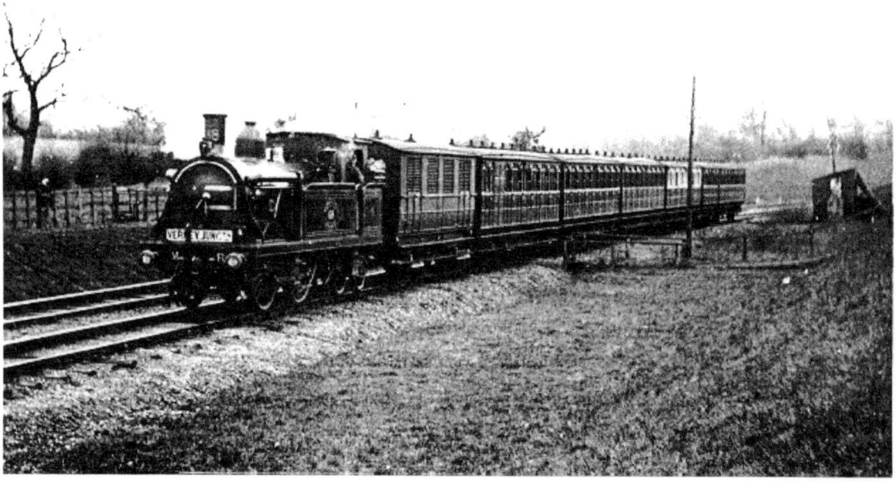

Class "C" No. 68 heads a Verney Junction train which includes a four-wheel van and a Pullman car. The date is prior to 1902 when a larger boiler was fitted.

Photo: L.U.R.S. Collection

Metropolitan "D" class 2-4-0T No. 75 at Neasden after removal of the condensing apparatus fitted when built but seldom used.

Photo: L.U.R.S. Collection

Hanbury resigned in November 1893 and the locomotive foreman at Neasden, T. F. Clark, was appointed in his place. The design of two 2-4-0T engines ordered from Sharp, Stewart & Co. in September 1894 with delivery in December, for use on the Aylesbury to Verney Junction line after the GWR terminated its working agreement, has been credited to Clark but they were very similar to engines produced by the same firm for the Barry Railway. Four more locomotives, delivered in May 1895, were fitted with condensing apparatus and had other detail differences but all six were classified "D".

In March 1897, primarily for shunting at Neasden, Peckett & Sons of Bristol supplied one of their standard 0-6-0 saddle tank engines and in November 1899 a second was ordered for similar duties in Harrow yard. Soon after arrival No. 101 was used on spoil trains during the construction of the Great Central line into Marylebone and in 1925 No. 102 spent a short time on hire to the District Railway but their duties were never arduous. They lasted into London Transport ownership, No. 101 as L.53 at Neasden and No. 102 (L.54) at Lillie Bridge depot.

Peckett saddle tank L.54 (Metropolitan No. 102) at Lillie Bridge depot
22nd June 1946 *Photo: H C Casserley*

As increased locomotive power again became necessary, Clark produced a modified version of the "C" class engines delivered five years previously. The cylinder dimensions remained the same at 17" dia x 26" stroke, as did the driving wheels, but boiler pressure was increased by 10 lbs to 150 lbs/in^2 and heating surfaces by about 25%. Tank and bunker capacities were also increased resulting in a total weight increase of about four tons. Two locomotives, Nos.77 and 78, were built at Neasden in 1896 followed by No.1 in 1898. In October 1898, although Clark had recommended that a further two locomotives should be built at Neasden, the directors invited tenders for four more. Hawthorn Leslie & Co. of Newcastle-on-Tyne were successful and Nos. 79 and 80 were delivered at the end of 1900 followed by Nos. 81 and 82 in April 1901. All seven were classified "E" although the cylinder diameter of the latter four was ½" larger than those built at Neasden. The original livery was similar to that of class "C" except that the words "Metropolitan Railway" and the number appeared on oval cast metal plates on the bunker. The next seven numbers, 83 to 89, were evidently intended for more class "E" locomotives not built due to the spread of electrification.

The "E" class locomotives were intended for use on passenger trains and, as goods traffic was also increasing, Clark designed a similar freight version. The tender of the Yorkshire Engine Company was accepted and four engines comprising class "F" were delivered in May 1901. They carried the same livery as the "E" class engines and, in similar manner, the condensing gear was soon removed and the bunker rails replaced.

Class "E" No. 81 as built by Hawthorn Leslie & Co. with condensing gear and coal rails topping the bunker. *Photo: L.U.R.S. collection*

What might have been! (see page 29) Class "F" No. 93 in LT livery as L.52 with (from left) Gerald Fitzgerald, James Stringer and an unknown colleague at Neasden in January 1963. *Photo: London Transport*

T. F. Clark resigned at the end of 1905, probably because of ill health, and was succeeded by Charles Jones who had been Electrical Engineer since 1903. After an attempt to acquire suitable second hand engines had failed, six firms were asked to quote to a broad specification prepared by Jones. Again the Yorkshire Engine Co. was successful and two 0-6-4 tanks were delivered at the end of 1915 followed by two more early in 1916 thus forming the "G" class. All four were given names, 94 - "Lord Aberconway" (Chairman of the Metropolitan), 95 - "Robert H. Selbie" (General Manager), 96 - "Charles Jones" and 97 - "Brill", the first Metropolitan steam locomotives to be named since the original Beyer Peacock tanks in the 1860's. They were painted in the usual deep red (known as Midcared) with black and yellow lining but with a single large panel containing the words "Metropolitan" and "Railway" in two curved lines above and below the Metropolitan crest. The locomotive number was on a plain rectangular plate on the bunker side. Following 97 two vacant numbers were left in the sequence leading to the suggestion, as with class "E", that more were to have been built.

"G" Class No. 97 "Brill" stands at Neasden awaiting its next duties.
Photo: L.U.R.S. Collection

Class "H" 4-4-4T No. 107 heads a morning train for Baker Street at Amersham, 22nd June 1935 *Photo: H C Casserley*

The continuing desire to accelerate timings led in 1920 to the introduction of the "H" class 4-4-4 tanks. It was stipulated that the class "G" boiler and trailing bogie were to be used and the engine was to be capable of negotiating curves of 4½ chains (99 yds or 93 metres) radius but detail design was left to the builders, Kerr Stuart & Company of Stoke-on-Trent. The engines were delivered, finished in the same livery as class "G", between October 1920 and June 1921 and subsequently handled most of the Metropolitan passenger services north of Harrow. They were reputed to reach 75 m.p.h. down Chorleywood Bank and the fastest trains reached Rickmansworth in 30 minutes and Amersham in 43 minutes from Baker Street.

In July 1923 the posts of Chief Electrical and Mechanical Engineers were separated, Charles Jones continued as CEE and George Hally was appointed CME and Works Manager at Neasden. To alleviate unemployment at Woolwich Arsenal at the end of the 1914-18 war, 100 2-6-0 tender engines of the SECR "N" class designed by R. E. L. Maunsell were ordered by the Government. 50 were sold to the Southern Railway as complete locomotives and the remainder, as sets of parts, went to the Great Southern Railway of Ireland (26 sets), Romanian State Railways (18) and the Metropolitan (6). The latter were sent to the Newcastle works of Sir W. G. Armstrong Whitworth & Co. where they were modified to the design of George Hally and emerged with lengthened frames, side tanks, bunker and a trailing bogie.

They entered service, designated class "K", in March 1925, painted in the final form of Metropolitan livery which was eventually applied to all surviving engines. This retained the single tank side panel but the two line lettering and crest were replaced by the single word "Metropolitan" which was in turn replaced by "London Transport" with the advent of the LPTB in 1933. Where cast plates were not fitted locomotive numbers were painted either centrally below the title or on the cab or bunker side with the Class letter immediately below.

The engines of classes "G", "H" and "K" were transferred to the Neasden ex-GCR shed on their sale to the LNER in 1937 and, after overhaul at Stratford works, were painted in an unlined black livery with LNER numbers (see Appendix II). Classes "G" and "K" remained at Neasden employed on Metropolitan line duties until withdrawn but the eight "H" class engines were transferred to Colwick, near Nottingham, in December 1941 where they were not really suitable for the heavier work expected of them and were consequently unpopular with both crews and maintenance staff. The surviving Metropolitan engines, comprising one class "A", four each of classes "E" and "F", and the two Peckett saddle tanks were renumbered in the "L.__" series.

A lull in shunting enables the crew to pose for the photographer beside "K" Class No. 111
Photo: L.U.R.S. collection

THE CENTENARIAN

HISTORY

In December 1897 Class "A" locomotive No. 1 was officially withdrawn from service in somewhat mysterious circumstances. According to an article by Alfred Rosling Bennett in the June 1908 edition of Railway Magazine:

> *" . . . she was scrapped owing to injuries received in the runaway accident at Baker Street, . . ."*

Several other sources repeat this information but the Railway Inspectorate of the Health and Safety Executive, responsible for investigating all railway accidents in Great Britain, have no record of any incident involving a Metropolitan engine at Baker Street which fits the information quoted.

Part 2 of Bennett's article, in the September issue, quotes an un-named correspondent as doubting this reason and suggesting that excessive rusting of the frames and horn-plates was to blame. In the absence of confirmation one way or the other the question will have to remain unresolved but what is beyond doubt is that the Metropolitan Railway Stores Committee met on 25th August 1897 to consider tenders from various firms for parts to build another *"new loco to replace No.1 now past repair"*.

The contract for *"1 pair locomotive engine frames finished complete in Siemens Martin mild steel"* was awarded to the Yorkshire Engine Company of Sheffield, whose bid of £64.0.0 with delivery in 8 weeks was preferred to those of Sharp Stewart, with a price of £55.0.0 but an 18 week delivery, and Beyer Peacock whose workers were on strike. 8 wheels at £26.0.0 per ton, a cranked axle at 69/- (£3.45p) per ton, 3 axles at 19/- (95p) per ton, and various other items were also purchased from Yorkshire Engine while the order for boiler plates and bogie frames went to the Leeds Forge Company, firebox plates were supplied by William Foster & Co. and the cylinders by Mr C. Duckering. The total cost was £2600 compared with £2081 each for Nos. 77 and 78, built at Neasden two years previously, and £3392 for each of the four built by Hawthorn Leslie.

In common with the other engines of the class, No. 1 was originally fitted with condensing apparatus, removed in about 1905, and trip-cocks, which operated to apply the brake if a signal was passed at danger. The two rails which topped the bunker were replaced by higher steel plates to increase the coal capacity and in about 1914 Westinghouse brake pump equipment was fitted. This was probably to enable electric stock to be shunted but it had been removed by 1930.

By 1908 the boilers of the Neasden built locomotives were giving cause for concern and three replacements were ordered from the Yorkshire Engine Co. at a total cost of £1483.10.0, No. 1 receiving one of these during a rebuild between August and December 1909. The cylinders were renewed in 1914 and again in 1929 while the boiler was exchanged in 1935 for the one carried previously by No. 82, after it had been repaired.

No. 1 at Neasden in the 1920's. The cylinder on top of the side tank is the reservoir for the Westinghouse brake. *Authors collection*

The seven Class "E" locomotives worked the majority of Aylesbury services until about 1916 and on the Chesham branch until the 1930s. Even after the LNER took over one was usually on stand-by at Rickmansworth and a letter to "Trains Illustrated", with a photograph of L.44 on an Aylesbury-Baker Street train in August 1952, commented *"Their spotless turn-out was a tonic contrast to the 'L1' 2-6-4 tanks"* usually employed. They were the engines used when Pullman cars were introduced on 1st June 1910, the Aylesbury service taking 28 minutes to reach Amersham and a further 23 minutes non-stop to Harrow, while the Chesham train took 36 minutes stopping at all stations, before both trains were electrically hauled to Aldgate or Liverpool Street respectively.

On 16th January 1902 the only Royal Train ever run by the Metropolitan conveyed King Edward VII the 24 miles from Baker Street to Amersham unchecked in 36 minutes after a delayed start due to the late arrival of the Royal party. Charles Ellis, in his report to the Board, made no reference to the composition of the train but it seems probable that a class "E" engine was used being the most modern passenger type available.

At the opening of the Uxbridge branch on 4th July 1904 No.1, adorned with flags and flowers, was the engine used to pull the special train, a duty repeated exactly fifty years later, as L.44, to celebrate the anniversary. On 22nd May 1955 L.44 headed a "Railway World" tour to Chesham and visited the town again on 10th September 1960 with a commemorative train carrying local dignitaries to mark the end of steam hauled passenger services on the branch, the last steam train was pulled by a BR class 2 2-6-2T the following night. Incidentally, the special train also provided LT with an illustration for their Christmas card that year.

L.44 again appeared on a passenger train with an afternoon tour for the Southern Counties Touring Society on 1st October 1961 leaving Wembley Park at 1.54pm for Stanmore, then travelling via Baker Street and Aldgate East to New Cross Gate on the East London Line where electric locomotive No.16 "Oliver Goldsmith" took over for the return to Baker Street at 4.04pm. The final LT appearance was at the Underground Railway Centennial celebrations at Neasden on 23rd May 1963 where L.44 headed a train consisting of a restored milk van, now in the London Transport Museum, and four ex-Metropolitan coaches owned by the Bluebell Railway.

"Railway World Special" passengers look on as L.44 is prepared in Chesham yard for the return to Baker Street, 22nd May 1955. *Photo: A J Reed*

NOTICE NO.84/64

LONDON TRANSPORT

METROPOLITAN, DISTRICT & PICCADILLY AND NORTHERN LINES

1. TRANSFER OF BATTERY CARS, EALING COMMON DEPOT TO LILLIE BRIDGE DEPOT
THIS EVENING WEDNESDAY 18TH MARCH

Battery cars, Nos. L55, L60 and L42 Ealing Common to Lillie Bridge.

Line Traffic Controller will arrange about 7.30 p.m.

Loco. Inspector Lillie Bridge will arrange crew.

2. TRANSFER OF LIGHT ENGINE, NEASDEN DEPOT TO COLD STORES SIDING, SKIMPOT LANE, LUTON (L.M.R.), BEDFORDSHIRE, 20TH MARCH

On Friday 20th March on behalf of "The London Railway Preservation Society Steam locomotive No.L44, will be transferred from Neasden (L.T.) to the London Midland Region and stable at private sidings at Luton, Bedfordshire.

Timings as follows:-

EX METROPOLITAN STEAM LOCOMOTIVE NO.44				
	A.M.			A.M.
Neasden depot (L.T.)	dep. 10.12	Willesden No.7	(arr.	11.52
			(dep.	11.54
				P.M.
Wembley Park	pass 10/20	Sudbury Jun.	(arr.	12.10
			(dep.	12.30
Harrow	pass 10/29	Watford Jun.	(arr.	1. 5 WATER
			(dep.	3.16 COAL (IF REQ.)
Harrow Yard	(arr. 10.31	Leighton Buzzard	(arr.	4.35 WATER
	(dep. 10.42		(dep.	4.45
Harrow	pass 10/44 To L.M.R.	Duhstable	(arr.	5.16
			(dep.	7.16
Neasden Sth Jun.	(arr. 10.58 WATER			
	(dep. 11.36			
Acton Canal Wharf	(arr. 11.46	Luton (Private Siding)	arr.	7.34
	(dep. 11.48			

Divisional Superintendent 'A' will arrange crews, and relief at Leighton Buzzard.

London Midland Region will provide the necessary Conductor crews.

Speed of the light engine will not exceed 25 m.p.h. throughout the journey.

3. TRANSFER OF STOCK, GOLDERS GREEN DEPOT - ACTON WORKS
FRIDAY 20TH MARCH

Four cars, 1938 Tube stock, Golders Green to Acton, in 'XX' timings.

Four cars, 1938 Tube stock, Acton to Golders Green, in 'XX' timings.

Divisional Superintendent 'B', to arrange crew.

4. TRANSFER OF STOCK, NEASDEN DEPOT - ACTON WORKS
FRIDAY 20TH MARCH

Seven cars, 1938 Tube stock, 12.29 p.m. ex Wembley Park.

Seven cars, 1938 Tube stock, 1.56 p.m. ex Acton Town.

Divisional Superintendent 'A', to arrange crew.

CONTINUED OVERLEAF

Details of the journey into preservation are sandwiched between routine stock movements on London Transport Notice No. 84/64.

Q.R.S. collection

PRESERVATION

In 1962 the last Class "F" 0-6-2T No. L.52 was withdrawn from service and two London Transport employees, craftsman Gerald Fitzgerald and apprentice James Stringer, presented a 50 signature petition to their employers requesting that it be placed on display at Neasden Works. They also sought assistance from the London Railway Preservation Society who showed little initial enthusiasm. However, when LT offered to sell the engine for preservation on another site after the Underground Centenary Celebrations at Neasden in May 1963, the LRPS agreed to help with publicity and accommodation but with no financial commitment. At that stage it was assumed that the engine was in good condition but subsequent correspondence revealed that the main frame was cracked and the maximum permitted boiler pressure had been reduced by 25%. In fact scrapping had been deferred for 12 months only to enable it to take part in the Centenary display and it was in no condition to steam on British Rail.

Attention then turned to the two remaining Class "E" locomotives recently withdrawn from service and, acting on LT advice, it was decided to purchase L.44 for £450. At the time the Metropolitan Tank Fund stood at only £40 with another £40 available from the LRPS but with the aid of a substantial loan from J H Tidbury, a generous supporter of the Society in its early days, the total was raised by the September deadline. Accommodation had been arranged at a private siding at Bishops Stortford in Essex but a ban on steam operations by British Railways, Eastern Region, forced a change of plan and on Friday, 20th March 1964 L.44 steamed out of Neasden depot bound for the Ministry of Supply cold store at Skimpot Lane, Luton, which was to be its home for the next 4½ years.

L.44 pictured under the wires of the West Coast main line at Leighton Buzzard on the way to Luton, 20th March 1964. *Photo: I Bowley*

In company with LNWR kitchen/diner No. 77 and other coaches, L.44 waits at Aylesbury before the six mile journey to Quainton, 23rd September 1970.
Photo: J M Hutchings

In October 1968 the Centenary of the Midland Railway London Extension was marked by an exhibition at Bedford and L.44 was invited to attend with the prospect of steaming on the Dunstable branch. Society members began preparing the boiler for a hydraulic test but enthusiasm waned when it was found that no exceptions would be made to the country-wide ban on steam operations imposed by British Rail, apart from "Flying Scotsman" which had its own contract. At the close of the event L.44, together with LNWR 1st class kitchen/diner No.77 and three Midland Railway goods vehicles, was moved to the sidings of International Alloys Ltd. at Aylesbury via Bletchley, Calvert and Quainton Road (non-stop).

Quainton Road Station was finally reached on 23rd September 1970 when the B.R. track was temporarily diverted into the down yard and all the stock from Aylesbury moved in. The priority at that time was the overhaul of the Society's other centenarian, LSWR Beattie well tank No.0314, and it was not until August 1975 that manpower and finance allowed a start to be made on L.44. With the cab, side tanks and boiler lifted off, the frames were jacked up and the wheels run out enabling worn surfaces to be renewed and the steelwork to be cleaned and repainted. New boiler lagging sheets and bunker extension plates were required as well as a lubricator to replace the stolen original but a hydraulic test did not reveal any serious problems with the boiler and it was hoped that all work would be completed by the Enthusiast's Weekend in September 1978. However progress was slow and, when a motive power crisis arose, priority had to be given to another ex-London Transport engine as L.99 was restored to its former guise as BR No. 7715.

Two cranes swing the boiler clear of the frames as restoration work proceeds at the Buckinghamshire Railway Centre in February 1976. *Photo: P I Clarke*

Although the wheels were re-united with the frames in 1979, little more was done in the next four years but then, to mark another new start, it was decreed that the engine would in future be known as "Metropolitan No. 1", L.44 was no more. The boiler was sent to Resco Ltd. of Woolwich for specialist repairs and, at Quainton, attention was given to cracked pistons, pitted cylinder bores and egg-shaped big-end journals. Over the next few months slidebars were realigned, crossheads repaired, eccentric straps remetalled and machined, piston rods and valve spindles ground and packed, a new back fitted to the cab and the side tanks repaired. When the boiler was returned on 16th March 1985 it was craned straight on to the waiting frames and No. 1 resembled a railway locomotive again!

Safety valves, injectors, firehole door, ashpan, blastpipe and blowers were soon added and, using an empty oil drum as a makeshift water tank, the boiler was steamed for the first time for twenty years on Saturday, 23rd March. Another steam test was carried out on the Sunday, mainly for the benefit of those who missed the first one, but unfortunately a leak developed at the regulator valve. The problem was sorted out overnight and early the following morning the fire was alight again in preparation for the final check by B.R. and insurance company inspectors.

By the end of March the boiler was lagged and the sidetanks and cab roof in place. A fortnight of intense activity by painters followed and, on 23rd April, No. 1 faced the Press in full Metropolitan livery, at least on the camera side! The fire was lit and No. 1 moved under its own power for the first time at Quainton, albeit as a 2-2-4 as the coupling rods were not fitted. A few minor problems were sorted out, the last brush strokes applied and, by the evening of Friday 3 May, all was ready for the celebrations planned for the following day.

Saturday dawned cold but dry and No. 1 took its place on Platform 3 at the head of a train made up of the 1901 built London & North Western Railway 1st class kitchen/diner No. 77 that had been its companion in store at Aylesbury 15 years previously, and an LNWR 6-wheel full brake dating from about 1890. By mid-day the sun was out and distinguished guests and sponsors were entertained to lunch and speeches before becoming the first passengers hauled by No. 1 for at least 20 years. The public relaunch took place on Monday, 6th May, when actor Don Estelle ("Lofty" of the television series "It Ain't 'alf 'ot Mum") arrived in a Locomobile steam car to break a celebratory bottle over the buffer beam and drive the train on its first "official" run.

The perseverance of the restoration team and the quality of their work was rewarded on 2nd April 1987 when the Buckinghamshire Railway Centre hosted the British Coal Heritage Awards and No. 1 made a spectacular entrance to be presented with the Award in the Rail category. *Photo: Bucks Herald*

Regular appearances on the demonstration track at Quainton Road were interspersed by visits to the Birmingham Railway Museum in June 1986, to work the Tyseley shuttle at their Gala Weekend, and in September 1987 to the Mid-Hants Railway's 10th Anniversary Festival of Steam where nearly 300 trouble free miles were covered in 16 days, double heading the "Watercress Belle" with the resident ex-SR "N" class No. 31874 and service trains with "S15" No. 506.

On 19th June 1989, No. 1 returned to Neasden works by road to prepare for the Chesham branch Centenary celebrations but unfortunately overheated an axlebox while on a test train to Watford leaving ex-GWR pannier tank No. 9466 to take over trains on the 1st and 2nd July. After a slow journey back to Neasden, the defective axlebox was removed and taken to the Festiniog Railway in North Wales for remetalling and machining. It was refitted the following Monday and, after surprising commuters with test runs to Ruislip and Uxbridge during the week, on Saturday, 8th July, exactly 100 years after the railway opened No. 1 steamed triumphantly into Chesham. The success of this event led to London Transport's "Steam on the Met" special trains between Harrow and Amersham in subsequent years. In 1990 the same two locomotives were involved and on 31st July No. 1 travelled round the Circle line on the way to an Open Day at Upminster, the first steam locomotive to work through the tunnels since its previous visit in 1961. On a final excursion away fron Quainton in April 1994, the curved 1 in 56 gradient out of Keighley station on the Worth Valley line gave No. 1 no trouble when its train of three ex-Metropolitan "Dreadnought" coaches and a Pullman revived memories of the Chesham branch of the 1930's and provided the subject for a second Christmas card!

No.1 pauses at St. James's Park on the way to Upminster in the early hours of 31st July 1990. *Photo: B Ammann*

A Christmas card from Yorkshire. No. 1 about to enter Mytholmes Tunnel on the Worth Valley line with a Metropolitan "Dreadnaught" coach.
From a watercolour by Clifford Meadway, courtesy R N Higgins

Over the years there have been many changes in the way railways are operated and regulations now in force decree that locomotives must be thoroughly inspected every ten years. No. 1 is now due for this statutory inspection and has been withdrawn from service until it can be carried out. The work involves completely dismantling the engine, examining, testing, repairing or replacing each component and reassembling everything to the satisfaction of inspectors appointed by the relevant authorities. The estimated cost of restoration to the standards demanded for main line use is £86,000, an interesting comparison with the price of a new engine 100 years ago!

Appendix 1

METROPOLITAN CHRONOLOGY

10 Jan 1863	Paddington to Farringdon opened
11 Aug 1863	Start of standard gauge working
23 Dec 1865	Farringdon to Moorgate opened
13 Apr 1868	Baker Street to Swiss Cottage opened
23 Sep 1868	Aylsbury & Buckingham Railway opened
1 Oct 1868	Paddington to Gloucester Road opened
24 Dec 1868	Gloucester Rd to South Kensington opened
1 Apr 1871	Wotton Tramway (Quainton Rd to Wotton) opened
Apr 1872	Wotton Tramway completed to Brill
7 Aug 1872	Sir Edward Watkin elected Chairman
1 Feb 1875	Moorgate to Liverpool St (GER) opened
12 Jul 1875	Liverpool St to Bishopsgate opened
18 Nov 1876	Bishopsgate to Aldgate opened
30 Jun 1879	Swiss Cottage to West Hampstead opened
24 Nov 1879	West Hampstead to Willesden Green opened
2 Aug 1880	Willesden Green to Harrow opened
25 May 1885	Harrow to Pinner opened
1 Sep 1887	Pinner to Rickmansworth opened
8 Jul 1889	Rickmansworth to Chesham opened
1 Jul 1891	Aylesbury to Verney Junction (A&BR) taken over
1 Sep 1892	Chalfont Road to Aylesbury (Brook St) opened
1 Jan 1894	Aylesbury (Brook St) to Aylesbury (GWR) opened
1 Apr 1894	Metropolitan local trains work to Verney Junc
1 Jan 1897	Baker St/Verney Jc through trains introduced
26 Jul 1898	Great Central opened for coal traffic
15 Mar 1899	Great Central opened for passenger traffic
1 Dec 1899	Wotton Tramway (Brill branch) taken over
13 Apr 1901	Death of Sir Edward Watkin
4 Jul 1904	Harrow to Uxbridge opened
1 Jan 1905	Electric trains introduced on Uxbridge line
23 Sep 1905	Electric trains introduced on Circle line
2 Apr 1906	Met & Great Central Joint Committee formed
1 Jun 1910	Pullman service introduced
5 Jan 1925	Electrification extended to Rickmansworth
1 Nov 1925	Watford branch opened
10 Dec 1932	Stanmore branch opened
1 Jul 1933	Formation of London Passenger Transport Board
30 Nov 1935	Brill branch closed
4 Jul 1936	Passenger service to Verney Junc withdrawn
1 Nov 1937	Metropolitan freight and passenger steam workings transferred to LNER
7 Oct 1939	Pullman service withdrawn
20 Nov 1939	Stanmore branch transferred to Bakerloo line
9 Sep 1961	Metropolitan services terminate at Amersham
20 Mar 1964	L.44 moved from Neasden to Luton
3 Sep 1966	BR (ex-GCR) line closed north of Aylesbury
30 Aug 1969	Opening of Quainton Railway Centre
6 Jun 1971	End of regular LT steam working
4 May 1985	No. 1 restored to service

Appendix 2

METROPOLITAN LOCOMOTIVES

No.	Type	Class	Coupled Wheels	Weight	Maker	Works No.	Built	Name	Date W'drn	Notes
1	4-4-0T	A	5' 9"	42T 03c	BP	412	1864	Jupiter	12/97	See Page 25
2	4-4-0T	A	5' 9"	42T 03c	BP	413	1864	Mars	-/07	(1)
3	4-4-0T	A	5' 9"	42T 03c	BP	414	1864	Juno	-/07	(1)
4	4-4-0T	A	5' 9"	42T 03c	BP	415	1864	Mercury	-/06	(1)
5	4-4-0T	A	5' 9"	42T 03c	BP	416	1864	Apollo	-/06	(1)
6	4-4-0T	A	5' 9"	42T 03c	BP	417	1864	Medusa	-/06	(2)
7	4-4-0T	A	5' 9"	42T 03c	BP	418	1864	Orion	-/25	(3)
8	4-4-0T	A	5' 9"	42T 03c	BP	419	1864	Pluto	-/07	(1)
9	4-4-0T	A	5' 9"	42T 03c	BP	420	1864	Minerva	-/06	(1)
10	4-4-0T	A	5' 9"	42T 03c	BP	421	1864	Cerberus	-/05	(4)
11	4-4-0T	A	5' 9"	42T 03c	BP	422	1864	Latona	-/05	(4)
12	4-4-0T	A	5' 9"	42T 03c	BP	423	1864	Cyclops	-/05	(4)
13	4-4-0T	A	5' 9"	42T 03c	BP	424	1864	Daphne	-/05	(4)
14	4-4-0T	A	5' 9"	42T 03c	BP	425	1864	Dido	-/05	(5)
15	4-4-0T	A	5' 9"	42T 03c	BP	426	1864	Aurora	-/05	(4)
16	4-4-0T	A	5' 9"	42T 03c	BP	427	1864	Achilles	-/07	(1)
17	4-4-0T	A	5' 9"	42T 03c	BP	428	1864	Ixion	-/07	(1)
18	4-4-0T	A	5' 9"	42T 03c	BP	429	1864	Hercules	-/26	(6)
19	4-4-0T	A	5' 9"	42T 12c	BP	706	1866		-/11	(1)
20	4-4-0T	A	5' 9"	42T 12c	BP	707	1866		-/05	(7)
21	4-4-0T	A	5' 9"	42T 12c	BP	708	1866		-/06	(1)
22	4-4-0T	A	5' 9"	42T 12c	BP	709	1866		-/25	(8)
23	4-4-0T	A	5' 9"	42T 12c	BP	710	1866		-/48	L45 (9)
24	4-4-0T	A	5' 9"	42T 12c	BP	770	1868		-/13	(10)
25	4-4-0T	A	5' 9"	42T 12c	BP	771	1868		-/13	(1)
26	4-4-0T	A	5' 9"	42T 12c	BP	772	1868		-/25	(2)
27	4-4-0T	A	5' 9"	42T 12c	BP	773	1868		-/35	Sold
28	4-4-0T	A	5' 9"	42T 12c	BP	774	1868		-/06	(11)
29	4-4-0T	A	5' 9"	42T 12c	BP	853	1868		-/25	Scrapped Neasden
30	4-4-0T	A	5' 9"	42T 12c	BP	854	1868		-/07	(1)
31	4-4-0T	A	5' 9"	42T 12c	BP	855	1869		-/06	(1)
32	4-4-0T	A	5' 9"	42T 12c	BP	856	1869		-/06	(1)
33	4-4-0T	A	5' 9"	42T 12c	BP	857	1869		-/06	(1)
34	0-6-0T	-	4' 0"	45T 00c	WE	35	1868		-/73	(12)
35	0-6-0T	-	4' 0"	45T 00c	WE	36	1868		-/73	(12)
36	0-6-0T	-	4' 0"	45T 00c	WE	37	1868		-/73	(12)
37	0-6-0T	-	4' 0"	45T 00c	WE	38	1868		-/75	(12)
38	0-6-0T	-	4' 0"	45T 00c	WE	39	1868		-/75	(12)
39	4-4-0T	A	5' 9"	42T 12c	BP	863	1869		-/06	(1)
40	4-4-0T	A	5' 9"	42T 12c	BP	864	1869		-/06	(1)
41	4-4-0T	A	5' 9"	42T 12c	BP	865	1869		-/36	Scrapped Neasden
42	4-4-0T	A	5' 9"	42T 12c	BP	866	1869		-/25	(1)
43	4-4-0T	A	5' 9"	42T 12c	BP	867	1869		-/13	(1)
44	4-4-0T	A	5' 9"	42T 12c	BP	868	1869		-/25	(2)
45	4-4-0T	A	5' 9"	42T 06c	BP	893	1870		-/06	(1)

No.	Type	Class	Coupled Wheels	Weight	Maker	Works No.	Built	Name	Date W'drn	Notes
46	4-4-0T	A	5' 9"	42T 06c	BP	894	1870		-/27	(6)
47	4-4-0T	A	5' 9"	42T 06c	BP	895	1870		-/06	(1)
48	4-4-0T	A	5' 9"	42T 06c	BP	896	1870		-/36	Sold
49	4-4-0T	A	5' 9"	42T 06c	BP	897	1870		-/36	Scrapped
34	4-4-0T	B	5' 9"	43T 15c	BP	1878	1880		-/05	(7)
35	4-4-0T	B	5' 9"	43T 15c	BP	1879	1880		-/06	(1)
36	4-4-0T	B	5' 9"	43T 15c	BP	1880	1880		-/06	(1)
37	4-4-0T	B	5' 9"	43T 15c	BP	1881	1880		-/05	(13)
38	4-4-0T	B	5' 9"	43T 15c	BP	1882	1880		-/07	(1)
50	4-4-0T	B	5' 9"	43T 15c	BP	1937	1880		-/07	(1)
51	4-4-0T	B	5' 9"	43T 15c	BP	1938	1880		-/11	(1)
52	4-4-0T	B	5' 9"	43T 15c	BP	1939	1880		-/07	(1)
53	4-4-0T	B	5' 9"	43T 15c	BP	1940	1880		-/07	(1)
54	4-4-0T	B	5' 9"	43T 15c	BP	1944	1880		-/06	(1)
55	4-4-0T	B	5' 9"	43T 15c	BP	1945	1880		-/06	(1)
56	4-4-0T	B	5' 9"	43T 15c	BP	1946	1880		-/07	(1)
57	4-4-0T	B	5' 9"	43T 15c	BP	1941	1880		-/07	(1,14)
58	4-4-0T	B	5' 9"	43T 15c	BP	1942	1880		-/11	(1,14)
59	4-4-0T	B	5' 9"	43T 15c	BP	1943	1880		-/11	(1,14)
60	4-4-0T	B	5' 9"	43T 15c	BP	2579	1884		-/07	(1)
61	4-4-0T	B	5' 9"	43T 15c	BP	2580	1884		-/07	(15)
62	4-4-0T	B	5' 9"	43T 15c	BP	2581	1884		-/07	(1)
63	4-4-0T	B	5' 9"	43T 15c	BP	2582	1884		-/07	(1)
64	4-4-0T	B	5' 9"	43T 15c	BP	2583	1884		-/07	(1)
65	4-4-0T	B	5' 9"	45T 04c	BP	2674	1885		-/11	(1)
66	4-4-0T	B	5' 9"	45T 04c	BP	2675	1885		-/05	(4)
67	0-4-4T	C	5' 6"	50T 08c	Ns	4352	1891		-/17	(16)
68	0-4-4T	C	5' 6"	50T 08c	Ns	4353	1891		-/23	(17)
69	0-4-4T	C	5' 6"	50T 08c	Ns	4354	1891		-/23	(17)
70	0-4-4T	C	5' 6"	50T 08c	Ns	4355	1891		-/23	(17)
71	2-4-0T	D	5' 3"	41T 04c	SS	4055	1894		-/20	(17)
72	2-4-0T	D	5' 3"	41T 04c	SS	4056	1894		-/16	(16)
73	2-4-0T	D	5' 3"	43T 10c	SS	4075	1895		-/20	(17)
74	2-4-0T	D	5' 3"	43T 10c	SS	4076	1895		-/21	(17)
75	2-4-0T	D	5' 3"	43T 10c	SS	4077	1895		-/21	(17)
76	2-4-0T	D	5' 3"	43T 10c	SS	4078	1895		-/21	(17)
77	0-4-4T	E	5' 6"	54T 10c	Ne	-	1896		-/62	L46
78	0-4-4T	E	5' 6"	54T 10c	Ne	-	1897		-/35	
1	0-4-4T	E	5' 6"	54T 10c	Ne	-	1898		-/63	L44
79	0-4-4T	E	5' 6"	54T 10c	HL	2474	1900		-/35	Sold
80	0-4-4T	E	5' 6"	54T 10c	HL	2475	1900		-/41	L47
81	0-4-4T	E	5' 6"	54T 10c	HL	2476	1901		-/63	L48 Scrapped Neasden 7/64
82	0-4-4T	E	5' 6"	54T 10c	HL	2477	1901		-/33	Sold
-	0-6-0ST	-	3' 1"	18T 00c	MW	616	1876	Wotton No.1	-/01	(18)
-	0-6-0ST	-	3' 0"	16T 15c	MW	1249	1894	Brill No.1	-/15	(19)
-	0-6-0ST	-	3' 0"	16T 15c	MW	1415	1899	Wotton No.2	-/15	(20)
90	0-6-2T	F	5' 2"	56T 00c	YE	624	1901		-/57	L49
91	0-6-2T	F	5' 2"	56T 00c	YE	625	1901		-/58	L50
92	0-6-2T	F	5' 2"	56T 00c	YE	626	1901		-/57	L51
93	0-6-2T	F	5' 2"	56T 00c	YE	627	1901		-/62	L52 Scrapped Neasden 7/64
94	0-6-4T	G	5' 9"	71T 07c	YE	1283	1915	Lord Aberconway	5/46	LNER M2 6154

No.	Type	Class	Coupled Wheels	Weight	Maker	Works No.	Built	Name	Date W'drn	Notes
95	0-6-4T	G	5' 9"	71T 07c	YE	1284	1916	Robert H Selbie	10/48	LNER M2 6155
96	0-6-4T	G	5' 9"	71T 07c	YE	1301	1916	Charles Jones	10/48	LNER M2 6156
97	0-6-4T	G	5' 9"	71T 07c	YE	1302	1916	Brill	1/43	LNER M2 6157
-	0-6-0ST	-	3' 0"	16T 15c	MW	23	1867	Nellie		(21)
100	0-4-0ST	-	3' 3"	22T 00c	HC	253	1886		-/07	(1)
101	0-6-0ST	-	3' 10"	39T 00c	Pe	664	1897		-/60	L53
102	0-6-0ST	-	3' 10"	39T 00c	Pe	823	1899		9/61	L54
103	4-4-4T	H	5' 9"	78T 05c	KS	4088	1920		3/46	LNER H2 6415
104	4-4-4T	H	5' 9"	78T 05c	KS	4089	1920		11/47	LNER H2 6416
105	4-4-4T	H	5' 9"	78T 05c	KS	4090	1920		10/47	LNER H2 6417
106	4-4-4T	H	5' 9"	78T 05c	KS	4091	1920		5/46	LNER H2 6418
107	4-4-4T	H	5' 9"	78T 05c	KS	4092	1921		9/43	LNER H2 6419
108	4-4-4T	H	5' 9"	78T 05c	KS	4093	1921		1/46	LNER H2 6420
109	4-4-4T	H	5' 9"	78T 05c	KS	4094	1921		4/42	LNER H2 6421
110	4-4-4T	H	5' 9"	78T 05c	KS	4095	1921		5/46	LNER H2 6422
111	2-6-4T	K	5' 6"	87T 07c	AW	702	1925		10/48	LNER L2 6158
112	2-6-4T	K	5' 6"	87T 07c	AW	703	1925		1/43	LNER L2 6159
113	2-6-4T	K	5' 6"	87T 07c	AW	704	1925		10/48	LNER L2 6160
114	2-6-4T	K	5' 6"	87T 07c	AW	705	1925		5/43	LNER L2 6161
115	2-6-4T	K	5' 6"	87T 07c	AW	706	1925		1/46	LNER L2 6162
116	2-6-4T	K	5' 6"	87T 07c	AW	707	1925		5/45	LNER L2 6163

Abbreviations:

AW - Armstrong Whitworth & Co., Scotswood, Newcastle-on-Tyne
BP - Beyer Peacock & Co., Gorton Foundry, Manchester
HL - Hawthorn Leslie & Co., Forth Banks Works, Newcastle-on-Tyne
KS - Kerr, Stuart & Co., California Works, Stoke-on-Trent
MW - Manning Wardle & Co., Boyne Engine Works, Leeds
Ne - Metropolitan Railway, Neasden Works
Ns - Neilson & Co., Hyde Park Works, Glasgow
Pe - Peckett & Sons, Atlas Engine Works, Bristol
SS - Sharp Stewart & Co., Atlas Works, Glasgow
WE - Worcester Engine Co., Worcester
YE - Yorkshire Engine Co., Meadowhall Works, Sheffield

Right: No. 1 brings up the rear as the train leaves Chesham station on the Centenary service to Watford on 8th July 1989. *Photo: A A Harland*

Notes:

Lxx Numbered in London Passenger Transport Board series from 1937
LNER Sold to LNER, 1st November 1937
(1) Sold to R.Fraser & Sons Ltd., Newcastle-on-Tyne as scrap
(2) Sold to R.Fraser & Sons Ltd., resold to Pelaw Main Colliery in 1926
(3) Sold to R.Fraser & Sons Ltd., resold to Mersey Railway (No.2) c1925
(4) Sold to Cambrian Railway, Nos.13 & 15 rebuilt as tender engines, all scrapped 1922/23
(5) Sold to South Hetton Colliery, rebuilt as 0-6-0T in 1908, scrapped 1948
(6) Sold to Sir Arthur Elvin as scrap
(7) Sold to Bradford Corporation (Nidd Valley Railway)
No.20 became No.1 "Holdsworth", scrapped c1920
No.34 became No.2 "Milner", resold to North Wales Granite Co. in 1914
(8) Sold to District Railway (No. 35), scrapped 1931
(9) Restored to 1903 condition, now in London Transport Museum, Covent Garden, London, WC2
(10) Sold to R.Fraser & Sons Ltd, resold to Birtley Colliery in 1922
(11) Sold to Sherwood Colliery
(12) Built for the St. John's Wood Extension line.
Nos.34, 35, 37 & 38 sold to Taff Vale Rly.
No.36 sold to Sirhowy Rly.
(13) Sold to A. King & Co., resold to West Somerset Mineral Railway
(14) Originally delivered to the South Eastern Railway, taken into Metropolitan stock in 1883
(15) Sold to Mersey Railway, scrapped 1925
(16) Sold to Ministry of Munitions
(17) Sold to Charles Williams, Morriston, S. Wales.
No.68 resold to Gwauncaegurwen Colliery Co.
No.74 resold to United National Collieries, Nine Mile Point Colliery, Cross Keys.
No.75 resold to Baldwins Ltd., Port Talbot (No.6) scrapped 1930
(18) Built 1876, originally named "Huddersfield", purchased by Oxford & Aylesbury Tramroad Co. in 1894, sold to Phillips of Newport, Mon. in 1901
(19) Supplied to O & A T in December 1894, originally named "Earl Temple", sold to T. W. Ward Ltd., Sheffield, resold to Frank Hayes of London
(20) Supplied to O & A T in February 1899, sold to T. W. Ward Ltd., Sheffield, resold to Holland, Hannen & Cubbitts
(21) Hired from Eckersley & Bayliss, 1907 to 1915 for light duties at Neasden

BIBLIOGRAPHY

Alliez, G: Engines of the Metropolitan Railway sold to Industrial Users, Railway Observer, November 1940

Baker, C: The Metropolitan Railway, Oakwood, 1951

Barker, T C & Robbins, Michael: A History of London Transport, George Allen & Unwin

Bennett, A Rosling: The Early Locomotive History of the Metropolitan Railway, Railway Magazine, June/Sept 1908

Bruce, J Graeme: Steam to Silver, Capital, 1983

Casserley, H C: The Later Years of Metropolitan Steam, Bradford Barton

Day, John: The Story of London's Underground, London Transport

Day, John & Fenton, William: The Last Drop, London Transport

Densham, P: Locomotives of the Metropolitan Railway, Denton Equipment, 1941

Dow, George: Great Central, Vol. 2: Dominion of Watkin, Locomotive Publishing, 1962

Foxell, Clive: Chesham Shuttle, 1996

Gadsden, E J S: Metropolitan Steam, Roundhouse, 1963

Goudie, Frank: Metropolitan Steam Locomotives, Capital, 1990

Harvey, Norman: Metropolitan Steam Locomotive Resume, Railway World, March 1961

Howson, H F: London's Underground, Ian Allan, 1951

Jackson, Alan A: London's Metropolitan Railway, David & Charles, 1986

Jackson, Alan A: The First Hundred Years, Chesham Town Council, 1989

Jones, Ken: The Wotton Tramway, Oakwood Press, 1974

Lee, Charles E: The Metropolitan Line, London Transport, 1972

Lee, Charles E: The Metropolitan in its prime, Railway Magazine, January 1963

Lee, Charles E: The Pioneer Underground Railway, Railway Magazine, February 1963

Locomotives of the LNER, Part 7, The Railway Correspondence and Travel Society, 1964

Locomotives of the LNER, Part 9A, The Railway Correspondence and Travel Society, 1977

Lowe, James W: British Steam Locomotive Builders, Goose, 1975

Page, T J: Metropolitan No. 1, Railway World, June 1984

Reed, Brian: Loco Profile, No.10: The Met Tanks, Profile, 1971

Simpson, Bill: The Brill Tramway, Oxford Publishing, 1985

Smith, Martin: Steam on the Underground, Ian Allan, 1994